I0779085

Tiny Little Cracks

Powerful Poems for
Your Pocket Collection

Bird's Eye View

Dr. Carol Graham

Staghorn Ridge Publications

Tiny Little Cracks
Powerful Poems for Your Pocket Collection:
Bird's Eye View

by Dr. Carol Graham

Author Contact Information:
E-mail: staghornridge@gmail.com

First edition published March, 2021

Library of Congress Cataloging-in-Publication Data

ISBN-13: 978-0-9861588-1-0
Library of Congress Control Number: 2021902603

Staghorn
Ridge
Publications
Harrison, ID

Dr. Carol Graham is a National Board Certified Reading and Language Arts Teacher Specialist. She is an elementary, middle school, and high school teacher, and principal. She worked as a teacher and principal for several decades in West Virginia.

As principal and a teacher at Hometown Elementary School in West Virginia, her leadership and experience spirited Hometown Elementary School to be recognized at the state and national levels. As a teacher, Dr. Graham's students achieved acclaim as finalists in a National NASA Competition and received several National STEM awards. During her tenure as principal, Hometown Elementary was selected as a National Green Ribbon School, a West Virginia State and National Title I Distinguished School, and a West Virginia School of Excellence. In addition, Hometown Elementary was selected as a winner in a national competition of the Washington, DC Kennedy Center for the Arts.

Beautiful Echo Ranch, near Kalispell, Montana, provided many childhood and young adult experiences for Dr. Graham. She fondly remembers riding her registered quarter horse, "Whimper Duke," many miles throughout the open range herding cattle. Later, she attended Montana State University to attain her degree in teaching.

Currently, Dr. Carol Graham teaches in the state of Idaho. Idaho has provided numerous additional interactions with students, parents, principals, and administrators. These opportunities, in addition to her wealth of experiences in West Virginia and Montana, provide the settings and backgrounds for her poetry, Children's books, and illustrations.

Gratitude in Grieving

Still the sweetness of her skin

I smell

Still the softness of her cheek

I feel

Still the steady assurance of her eyes

I see

Still the lightness of her laughter

I hear

But when I turn around

She's not there

Spent Spring

And there it was
November

In June no one thinks
about November

The only thing you think about
In June is July

In July everyone thinks
August will be hotter

But in August we all know
September brings school

And October pumpkins

Yet when November arrives

No one knows

What happened to the year!

Nature Unfolds Slowly

When spring came

A new branch was on the tree

It stood out because it was long

Too, too long

Clipping it came to mind

But then a thought came

Maybe it is a branch that

Guides others how to grow

Is it a mindset, to think

That a branch is too long?

So, I decided to watch

And wait, and then wait longer

When the next spring came

I looked for that same branch

It was then that I noticed

That it was no longer too long!

Still Standing

Brilliant sunshine streaming
Pine green needles abound
Softly hobbles a speckled fawn
Rustling squirrels scatter 'round

Deformed branches hang low
Snapped twigs now spent
Gnarled scars clearly visible
Past winters leaving dents

Courageously standing
Despite repeated harsh snows
Threatening calamity
With each decisive blow

Tiny Little Cracks

Still upright but leaning

Weathering a peaceful serenity

Sordid spells of impelling disaster

Continues thrashing its identity

Skies clear once again

Birds flit to the boughs

Carefree days passing by

Such as life somehow.

The Flame Most Bright

A flame burns most brightly

Just before it goes out

No one knows exactly

How this comes about

Perhaps the flame knows

And able to anticipate

The coming total darkness

Therefore, does not hesitate

The knowledge that we have

Is not so profound

To guide this understanding

Continues to astound

Tiny Little Cracks

Loved ones stirred to see

Sickness disappears

Heartbreak overcome

When the flame is near

Burn your light the brightest

The glow will carry on

Rest in others resoluteness

Before your light is gone

The Jay and the Gray

There they glared, the jay and the grey

A fat peanut between and neither giving way

A high- pitched screech, violent twitching tail

Puffed up fur, rough feathers then flailed

Bushy fur flew, feathers strung sky high

Round they went, while the peanut sat by

Along came a snail, not so fast, you know

Taking its time, far as snails go

The battle went on, and the snail did too

The only difference was that peanut was chewed

The hullabaloo over, what laid upon the ground

The brittle pieces, is what the two now found

This simple tale might seem quite trite

But the bird and the squirrel

Learned not to fight

Separation

A child is like a leaf

Struggling to be free

Swaying in the breeze

Clinging to a tree

Tiny but so green

Passing time will tell

Sustaining life itself

But only for a spell

Gently breaking free

One autumn windy day

Pausing as it drifts

Passing as if to say:

Thank you, mother tree

I'm not going far

I'll settle at your feet

You are my shining star!

The Weed

Tall and straight

Amongst the elegant stems

Swaying in unison

Soft breezes blend

Perched in the shadow

But closely lies

Another much stronger

Reaching sunny skies

Perhaps it knows

It's much better to hide

Then standing taller

Those prettier than I

Should I be noticed?

Fortunately, not so

Another day passes

So, I can grow.

Once

Yellowed clippings

Adorn plastered aged walls

Unknown scribblings

Scattered and small

Aged names and places

Conveniently described

Younger generations passing

Musing questions of why?

Encompassing greatness

Meticulously displayed

Devoid of all beauty

Tattered remnants remain

Disappearing significance

Evaporates each day

Potential survivors

Passing slowly away

Historical importance

Held dearly to none

Drifting towards oblivion

Once special to one.

Good Lesson

Early this morning

Before the break of dawn

Grazing alone in a field

Frolicked a spotted fawn

Seeming unsure

Sniffing at the spring grass

The fawn became startled

When a butterfly danced past

Distracted at once

But delighted to see

He followed the fluttering

Discovering a tree

Tiny Little Cracks

Bumping his head

At the stout piece of wood

Backing up to admire

Yet, not quite understood

'Round about then

Mom scampered to aid

That inquisitive fawn

She calmly surveyed

Walking slowly away

Glancing quickly to find

Her frolicking fawn

Lurching past her behind

Prancing and pawing

That fawn having such fun

Finally, Mom decided

To join her happy son

Together they darted

It was so clear to me

Perhaps, we should take the time...

To bump into a tree!

The Thing About A Puddle

The problem with a puddle

That mothers seem to know

Is that they're good for nothing

And children do not outgrow

Instructions are given early

Mothers pleading to the child

"Do not step in any puddles."

Not usually with a smile

The child listens intently

Remembers the sharp "No" word

But more often than expected

The word "fun" is being heard

Puddles are like magnets

They have a mysterious pull

Calling all children…

"Come in...I'm deliciously full

The water is so pleasant

Your feet will stay dry

Step in to the wonderous power

Come, come give me a try!"

The calling of a puddle

Will always over-ride a plea

Determined opposition

Children think about "ME!"

Tiny Little Cracks

Puddles bring laughter

Puddles make them smile

Children can't resist them

Even when put on trial

"Why didn't you listen?"

I've said it once, again

Your shoes and socks are wet

Yet still you jump on a whim!'

Next time you see a puddle

Consider these points of view

Whether you step in it

The choice is still up to you!

The Truth About Writing

Often when I write

The words are in my eyes

Then jump upon the paper

Much to my surprise

It does not help to struggle

Meddling or to strain

Simply gazing out the window

They seem to come in rain

The Arrangement

January came one year

Hope hung by its coattail

Peace prospered under rule

Mountain ranges stood tall

Then the people parted

Mercy departed and wailed

Voices rising in protest

The tide has turned

Love lies beneath cold hearts, slumped
shoulders

In a moment on an ordinary day

Where the chattering chipmunk sings

Apple blossom fragrance sweetly floats
upon the misty foggy morning

In a moment on an ordinary day

If grasping of the fleeting time

Can be recognized as a glimpse

Never wrapped the same to witness

This moment on an ordinary day

Is here just this once to touch

Embrace the wonder of the instant

As it quickly leaves our clutch

I Think I Helped a Worm Today

I think I helped a worm today
Yet know I not for sure to say
Quiet it lay upon the road
Riddled in grit for it had slowed

Bent did I to see it twitch
As water flowed beside a ditch
Plucked to moisten in my hand
Freeing tiny bits of sand

Gently on the grass I placed
Holding breath aback I braced
Intent of which I yearned to see
Yet know it might not be

High Potential

Indeed, I read the scholars' work

Kept their expressions close

Rather harsh critics of others' effort

Is one thing I noted most

On one hand an open reflection

Productive, but then some joke

Presenting a different direction

Sending the intent up in smoke!

"Aesthetically challenged" wrote one

About another's verse

"What does this author believe or think?"

The comments became even worse

Setting aside the materials

Society elitists of fame

I decided to write this poem

Hoping one day I have the same!

Green Went the Garden

Today my garden went green
As Life sprang from the ground
Yet shades of shadows seen
Slowed the shoots, I fear, down

Grand scenes of gorgeous gowns
Scalloped tulip skirts crown
Azure eggs speckled clowns
The sights and sounds astound

Gasps swiftly a strong gust
Slicing stems through so green
Reminds startups "adjust!"
Yet all seems so serene!

One Day

There is a time

One comes to face

No longer lingering

Leaving no trace

The things that needed

Your special touch

Await another

Consumed so much

Fresh and eager

To change the world

Through the storms

Strength unfurled

Abruptly comes

The final call

Former pictures

On the wall

Their names beneath

A framed bygone

Approaching the end

Towards a new dawn

Unleashing the Load

Is there such a thing as knowing?

What will happen if I try?

Will there be a resolution?

Or will fear succumb to why?

I have taken this path beforehand

Thoughts that time would surely tell

That the love for one another

Erase the hurts that once befell

Yet again, I was mistaken

Revenge and hatred rose once more

Anger surfaced from confusion

Leaving me outside the door

Thinking

When you have no snow to shovel

Or rotting leaves to rake

Nor simple seeds for planting

And nothing decent to bake

Where nary a load of wash

Needs hung upon the line

No muss of dust to linger

Not possible things are fine

Are tasks to do required?

What if we had not one?

Might these formations

Intent to steal time in the sun?

Perhaps, such endless toil

Could be set aside to wait

While sitting in an armchair

As I contemplate!

He Did Not Know

Thoreau could not have known

His quiet nuances

And constant nudgings

Driven scribblings

Could finally cause

A deliberative call to change.

I Saw This Tree

The gnarled branch

Encrusted in dried sap

Gaping dark holes

Held tiny restful places

For creature cradled naps

An examination more fine

Revealed beneath the vines

Peering directly at me

Apparently, not frightened to flee

And I, no longer interested to see

No Doubt

It's safe to say when autumn comes

The corn won't be in

And the hay won't be done

The garden won't be hoed

And the cows will be out

The fence not mended

And the stalks are in doubt

All the food stuffs empty

And the fields unplowed

Though the biting winds cut

Through my thin thread shroud

Stinging tear streaked eyes

While blistered hands work

Yet the work will endure

And the time needed in doubt

The snow will still settle

And the cows still out

The Sorel Solution

I never knew what a SOREL was

I had never heard the name

But since buying "Winter Fancy- Tall

I will never be the same.

The fit, the color and style

Gives my appearance a lift

The cut and Oh, so comfy

I feel I've received a gift!

Finally Found

Crush one's spirit flat

Sometimes seems a bit harsh

When quiet signs are ignored

The Overseer exacts more force

Sifting still unbridled peace

Strenuous to uphold

Changing time, begging decision

Yet eventually a few

Become quite adapt at…

Listening for what is true

And finally learn…

And when they DID, they grew

Stepping Back

All have been selected

Not without a fight

Words poorly chosen

Hurts flung with might

Can we overcome?

Painful remembrances sown

The challenge laid before us

As we move through the unknown

Wisely "hope" was mentioned

By leaders known so well

If we take heart and solace

All, will end, time will tell

Kindergarten Kids

In the quiet of the classroom

All, were hard at work

Writing all their letters

Sounding out new words

Cameron, had stopped crying

Blake, no longer hit

Justin, looked me in the eye

Lilly, had finally quit.

But something beautiful had happened

That, I just have to tell…

In Kindergarten on that day,

ALL had turned out well.

The Clarity of Clara

Clara did not know

That Albert held her hand

Memories flowing like golden baubles

Yielding a peaceful plan

Through the tireless trauma

Selfless caring concerns

She steadfastly walked beside him

Facing the perilous turns

Finality fleeing with precision

But Clara was dutifully prepared

Her suitcase packed, she stated

"Albert, dear, I'm climbing the stairs."

Passing Through

Chomping the lush spring grass

Nervously glancing sideways looks

Moving onward hesitantly, expectantly

All knowing the destination

Except me.

Their movements giving the direction

Not revealing the goal

Yet they know…disappearing from sight

Leaving wonder and astonishment

Behind …for me.

Which Way?

If I was sure to wonder, why

It is possible not to stretch high?

For certainty stops, at the front door

But unsureness, fills the desire for more

More of what…I often ask?

Not wanting a single day to pass

Embracing the new...shy away, no?

Is the direction...frightful though?

For if I knew, where that path led

'Tis the possibilities, to dread?

Unknown wanderings, grace befall?

Awaits those not limited, by solemn walls.

Loyal followers of the thrill

Succumb to drudgery up the hill

For ones inclined to be put in place

Foregoing an often, heated race

Awkwardness, failure runs, too deep

Yet wisdom reveals...oh so sweet!

If Not for Mindfulness

I met tomorrow after living today

Focused on the present abruptly blocking the way

Planning all my actions, thoughts, and words

Avoiding coming sorrow, I knew not what to say

Being fully present, drains the brain, you see

Mindful occupation is somewhat, agony

The impact of the moment… stresses continuity

"Tomorrows," left a-wandering…sailing out to
sea.

Perhaps it is better to ponder now and then

Generally, tomorrow will again appear

The present holds the candle they say…

But tomorrow, manages the fear

What of This Earth Matters

And what of this earth matters to us

bloodied bodies –

animal and human?

For what deeds, so wrong and unjust

struck down because. . .

they breathe?

Not like us but, are they really,

if. . .we see us in them?

The Ball

It was an Airball

But I did not know

A Lay-Up…

For me to grow

Later a Rebound

Removing the false Screen

Together a "Swish"

Providence unforeseen.

When Your Brother Comes In

When your brother comes in

That's when we'll eat dinner

Chickens, cows, and pigs need fed

Done with that… you can peel potatoes

Your sisters are finishing the pies

Dad is coming home soon

Set the table and the good silverware

Cranberries need a lid on them

Why are you looking at me?

Thanksgiving is when we're home.

Forever Found

A humble heart stowed away

Slumbers sweetly in peace

Broken pieces held by none

Sown together once again

Withered wilted gentle spirit

Rise to do no more

Courage resting unadorned

Drum-beats, silenced still

Overcome feelings frozen in time

Faded features weather worn

Yellow glass frames memories

Forever found within

Knight of the Night

Part the clouds, to create a chasm

Peel the darkness back to see

Save the gift of enthusiasm

Sound the wind, to sway the trees

Wait and will the guiding moon

Make its mark a sight of wonder

Behold the silence, swift and soon

Translucent waves pound like thunder

Suddenly stillness creeps and crawls

Drowning ascending frothy debris

Like a knight a single performer

Casting a muse to crown the sea

Subjugated

There was a man
His name was Frank
He seldom spoke
And he never drank.

He lived alone
Outside of town
No one knew
What he had found.

He did not gossip
For naught to tell
So, folks never knew
His life was swell.

The less he spoke
The more they did
Prying to know more
Just how he lived.

What religion was he?
Did he believe?
Since they didn't know
They perceived.

He must be changed…
be more like us
worried about others,
when one doesn't fuss.

First Light

Will the sun come up tomorrow?

Daylight to chase away the night...

Can assurance from the past

Bring forth the warmth and light?

Behind majestic mountains-

Beyond horizons not in view

Perhaps it rests behind the moon

Painting tomorrow's skies anew!

Then There Was Chaos

Unexpected encounter on an ordinary day

In an ordinary setting

Doing ordinary things

Worlds apart...until that moment

Unseen forces acting as magnets do

Atoms stopped in their tracks-

On that ordinary day...

Not Ordinary

If it was not for tomorrow

Could we live a life today?

Would the day be as inviting?

If tomorrow went away?

Momentarily

Even still the bee hums

When frosty branches hang

Finding the last drop of nectar

The last moment before...

Soon

Where does the water wander?

Does it know the path?

I will know the answer

When I find my own

This Day

I only took a moment

Remembering what I read

Early up this morning

Re-reading words once said

As the day continued

Much to my surprise

Amazing things unfolded

Right before my eyes

Rain weakened, then subsided

Cluttered clouds left the sky

Short of a couple hours

The sun streamed forth on high

Pleasantries piled upon me

From people not found before

My steps became much lighter

Blessings bubbling up galore

The work-day was a breeze

And when the end was near

I sat that book beside me

To hold those words so dear.

The Hooves Under the Montana Moon

There happened a scene in the dark of night

By a girl who dreamed bold

The Montana range can quickly change

And this secret must be told

The Montana gravesites have seen gunfights

But the girl escaped this grip

T'was to outflank on the Crystal Lake Bank

Competing in gamesmanship

Now this young girl was born and raised

Stubborn, daring, threefold

Why to decide to ride astride that Shetland

No one knows

She was always bold, but forever told not to…

Unbridle the horse

But her cousin stayed that's when she strayed

Charting this horrible course

On a hot summer's eve both agreed to deceive

They're whereabouts at dusk

Talk of the hear, they planned their feat

Brimming with mistrust

Saddles thrown no bridles sown on…

Either horses' back

As twilight loomed they gave a nod

Then there was a crack

Long legs flailed while short ones railed

As the Shetland strove to reach

Tiny, the horse took the course

Like an animal beseeched

Stars overhead as they sped….flying

Through the night

Without a rope she had no hope

Of steering her quite right

The worst last need is a thing to heed

Taking your last breath

Yet gasping for air neither foul nor fair

Trampled half to death

Bet on they went 'til horses were spent

Slinking through the cabin door

Both settled back the night was black

But the girl was dreadfully sore

Bravely in the light on that crisp night

In the warmth of the roaring fire

With a sort of moan and then a groan

She felt a keen desire

Her eyes grew wide for on the inside

A hoof print squarely dwelled

Centered on her chest causing such distress

Bloodied, bruised befelled

At the streak of dawn the bet was gone

The secret to behold

The awful dread nothing was said

Beneath the denim told

The leather chaps lighthearted slaps

Whimpers left unsaid

But the searing pain was to remain

The adventure to be read

At the Dinner Table

At the dinner table trouble lurked…

Often a place for sharing and reminiscing

Good times…funny happenings

Only known to familiar participants

Chuckling abounded between mouthfuls

Good natured prodding…at catastrophes

Often preceding the moments of interjection

I won't do that again…or maybe…

Next time when that…

There never was a next time…

Tales evolved about events as time wore on

That may…or may not have occurred

Pertaining to the member that was "accused'

…of the mishap

True to transpire the common theme…

Inexperience youth and age

No matter….responsibility must be "owned up to"

Fixing, rebuilding, reworking, resolving…

Whining. not heard of…

At the dinner table

When the Needles Fall

When the needles fall
Tamaracks wear brilliant yellow
Air takes on a bitter chill
Sunsets fade and mellow

Black bear sporting heavy coats
Thundering elk are heard
Browns and golds glisten in the sun
Changing seasons have stirred

Ranchers mounted on their steeds
Horses chaffing at the bit
Time in the saddle turns to days
Gentle light on paths moonlit

Montana boasts of azure skies

But winters 'round the bend

Deep snows and blustery winds

Beckoning like a good friend

Cattle herds are here and there

Open range extending for miles

Numbers checked against the spring

"Hope" resting amongst the trials.

Sea of Storms

When thunderous storms abruptly…

Carve memories into time

Changing routines sharply

Transforming humankind…

Once backyard conversations…

In summer's sweet shade

Beneath the spreading branches

Swiftly fallen then laid

Strewn across the fences…

Branches shattering the calm

Disaster wreaking havoc..

Roots upward bound

Unsettled next direction

Needs clamoring to be filled…

Smatterings of kindness

Folks appearing… as if willed

Bringing forth good cheer

Reassurance comes to past…

Lifting shattered spirits

Thankfulness at last!

Shaped by a Shetland

Pixie barred his big white teeth

Planting hooves sternly in the grass

Grounded in amongst the herd

Blinded by events of the past

Remembering behavior tried and true

Quickly learning tricks of the trade

The goal to remain with the others

If quite enough trouble is made

The battle to remain in the pasture

No bridle was "HE" going to wear

No galloping with a rider aloft

Prepare and hence the warfare

If barring the teeth doesn't work

Charging forth with madness might

Planting hooves deeply thrusted

Frightens all humans downright!

Not much past the age of nine

Sheltered by a sturdy rail fence

Gathering courage best mustered

Threatening a desperate defense

A prolonged stare encountered

Neither throwing the gauntlet down

A youngster determined to ride

I hunted my father…'til found

Tiny Little Cracks

Peering at his eyes from on high

Wondering if this was the same horse

Amazed at the difference a father can have

Changing the attitude and this discourse

Steadfast Sunshine

Silently the snow blankets the ground

Squirrels chattering "beware"

Jays gobbling the corn

Before taking wing with despair

Spotted chipmunks nestled.... doors barred

Biting wind cannot break in

He's pounding at their tiny huts

Drifting sleep dousing the din

After the conference in December

The eagles agreed they must go

Toppled treetops strewn about

Highlighted in the memo

Trees hanging with exhaustion

Hugging each other for support

Crusty snow spread so thickly

Darkening days becoming short

The sun, determined, takes a stance

Persuading the mighty grounding fog

Peeking through the melancholy gloom

Refashioning nature's dialogue

Snowball Rule

You'd better put that down!
Mike yelled to Fred
Mrs. Cox told us yesterday
That's what she said
"No snowballs ever!"
"Not even if it's soft!"
It might be wet
But she still said "Naught"

"Naught," that's the word
I'm not sure what it means
I didn't raise my hand
'Cause she says "I dream"
She thinks I don't listen
But I try real hard
I'm trying to get better
'Cause she's "in charge"

What exactly did she say?

Mmm…let me think…let's see…

We'd better not be caught

She wasn't lookin' at me

I'm not exactly sure

But were 'sposed ta' know

You've done it enough..

Now let me throw!

Orchard's Folly

Harry, once was a man on the run

Losing his mind with a gun

Governor Frank

Lost his rank

Now both lay under the sun

The Ballad of the Pendulous Penn

During many dark nights, Lyda spoke the last rites

    Over the men betrothed then loathed

Her talons dove, as relatives strove

    Illuminating her greed clothed

The Old Idaho Penn was no playpen

    Some thirteen thousand inmates all told

No woman surpassed, Lady Bluebeard's past

    Such scandals she denied but bankrolled

The women's ward was built you see

    With a wall 'round the old warden's home

Until then, women served time with men

    As the story goes

If you visit today, inmate's writings might say

Thoughts experienced in "Siberia," or the
"Cooler"

Lyda got ten years to life, escaped in the night

    Probably not through the sewer

The "Outlaws" played teams, without any means

    Maybe with a fellow named "Scarface"

The Rose Garden forthright, was historically the site

    On which six hangings took place

Yet their debts have been paid, all are now laid

    The Old Idaho Penn left no trace

My Teacher Said

My teacher said that I could be

President of this great country

As a citizen I solemnly vow

To uphold the constitution somehow

I learned about Washington D.C.

The poem on the Statue of Liberty

The battles fought for our great land

How representation came to stand

Manifest Destiny and the search for gold

How the American Indians land was sold

Equal rights existed for only some

Blood was shed and slaves did run

When the institution of slavery fell

The strife of getting our country well

Industrialization and women's rights

How youngsters like me worked day and night

My mother told how banks had closed

How Roosevelt's Deal gave jobs to those

The wars for freedom that were fought

Women worked on jobs they sought

Martin Luther had a dream

President Johnson served this team

Even though we have equal rights

Blood still fell in more great fights

Yet our president of today

Represents our country's good and bad days.

Whimper Duke

That quarter horse gelding was
A beautiful cinnamon brown
Bright, inquisitive gaze
Two-year hooves settled down

He is quite "green"
Was the word given to Dad
Not ready to saddle
We didn't know what we had

Later when saddled
Against the azure Montana sky
Whimper Duke stood magnificently
Dad decided to give him a try

At first, calm with the saddle

Seemingly with nothing amiss

For a few brief moments

That horse was all sweetness and bliss

Settling in the seat of the saddle

He reared back his great head

Flailing hooves struck out blindly

Aghast we had been misled

The next moments as I recall

Danced by in a complete blur

Enfolding mayhem then ensued

This situation then occurred

A bellow sprang from his throat

Hunching his back in an arc

Dad was thrown high in the air

This was only the start

Hooves appeared everywhere

Gnashing teeth strained to grasp

Lunging simultaneously at all

Through the split rail at last

When the dust finally cleared

Debris strewn about the ground

We peered anxiously behind barriers

Shaking as he snorted us down

Charging at the wooden rails

Aiming his big white teeth towards us

We fled hurriedly from sight

No confidence in wood did we trust

A day or two passed

Much conversation took place

No one dared to attempt

Ranch life moves at its own pace

Twenty years have plowed by

Surprises never did subside

That horse showed his independence

With a glimmer in his eye

His name will not be forgotten

Nor the antics that he displayed

I'm glad to be able to relate it

Thank goodness that I had prayed

Just Enough Time

Years turn to decades

Decades gone by

Slowly passes quickly

Things go awry

The life that was planned

Didn't happen as it should

Thinking about the past

Often becomes understood

Decisions that were made

Didn't turn out right

Some do not recover

Some reach new heights

What is the difference?

Between these two results

Why do some rediscover

While others add to insult

All have similar quests

Some folks become devout

Sad to say though

Often when time's run out

Some wish they had

More time to breakout

Had done what they wanted

Instead of selling out

Afraid to ask

No courage to try

They let their dreams go

They let time slip by

At the end

Before saying goodbye

Unfulfilled dreams return

Regrets then underlie

Unjust Sagacity

The counselor said, "You'll never make it,'

thrusting the results forward with a
period…imprinting

the comment permanently within the young
synapses

developing within.

The matter-of-fact presentation

was surely…

a solidly accurate insight of the

highly-educated adult sitting forthright.

The intensity of the remark delivered

with the boldness and assuredness

of a seasoned and respected elder

received respectively with all of the
credibility…

that a 16 year old can muster

Finality set…

before the youngster…

setting the bar before the bar is fathomed

capping the future of the young.

Hence determining the destiny

of a child.

But They Lived

The passing of one so loved

Cannot be held within

A life so full… so generous

Seems to dwell but then

The conscious mind reminds the times

Clinging to the soul

Reality abruptly leaps

Gripping a heart so whole

Fighting entwined memories

Cherishing…once so real

Suppressing brutal truths

Grasping not to feel

Side by side each day

Breathing each other's breaths

Ending the other's sentence

Oneness in such depth

Backward thinking vanquish

Why…how…should

Linger but subsiding

Wishing for the "could

Unsettling thoughts behold

Proceeding but not cured

Emptiness encompassing

Destiny not assured

A crack so deep…so broken

A lifetime spoken gone

Closing eyes, reset the time

Once again 'till dawn

Clemency Contingence

I've heard it said "time will tell,'

Well-meaning acquaintances comfort

But no guarantee is aligned to insure forgiveness,

Mercy and grace will emerge

Perhaps souls mellow…misunderstandings subside

Understanding broadens…

Days gone by....passing

Without interruptions absorbing reflection

Criticism, indignation, accusations linger

Softened by the creeping peace of silence…

Troubles, no longer needing first place

Perspective at last…

It's lonely face peering gently from the obstruction

Of words hastily bespoken

Yokes of Understanding

The study of man from a woman's point of view

Seems complicated, but some differences
appear to be poignant

When the occasion arises and a woman needs
assistance

She's not afraid to ask someone, but on the
other hand, a man absolutely takes a pass

A man will persistently grasp the wheel all day
long, going the wrong way, refusing any
guidance and definitely taking an issue,
opposing all correction that might point to a
different venue, bound and determined to solve
the task at hand

The woman, however, doesn't understand

Seeing that it does no good to argue…

That's an issue too…

Whatever the woman suggests, it is bound to be
wrong and, for sure, it isn't "logical"

Explaining it, even with higher volume, does appear to clarify to some degree, like red-pursed up faces in frustration, is the answer

Then the woman melts, sealing the deal of weakness, when in reality it is a sign of calling in for assistance…

The man just wonders why the woman can't 'get it,' denying any guilt that might creep in

Neither likely to get results

Chair of Courage Past

"Walking in nature frees the soul...," the excerpt read in bold print

I pondered the phrase for a moment, reflecting upon the flattened, rotted dead leaves strewn about on the ragged, once well-worn path adjacent to the spectacle of a garage

Peeking around the overturned rusted wheelbarrow precariously, leaning against the splintered picket barrier of a fence, appeared the "Path of Enlightenment," I was sure

Slipping past the rusted-out water cooler Gramps used for angling, I wound through the briars, behind my neighbor's dilapidated Volkswagen

"Not free yet...," I thought, pushing onward to uncover the profound happiness that had been missing in my soul, discovering the warm blood trickling downward soaking my crumpled favorite shirt

Thrusting the razor blade thorns aside, forcing an
opening in the dense thicket pressing my torso
against the branches of sublime bliss I was not yet
embracing, but sure to befall me from my
determined perseverance

Then suddenly, flopping headlong atop a twisted
wooden mass of nothingness my soul lurched

Jutting upward the sharpest of pangs ravaged
against my ribcage stealing my gasping breath

Rolling sideways then stumbling to a stooped
position

Fumbling to recognize my way, back-tracking
through the chaos

Piercing pains over-riding the longing desire for
adventure

Drawing myself to the closest available place of comfort minus pain, I crawled across the floor gripping the cuts and abrasions I had just incurred

Flopping damaged appendages while groaning and wincing, I toppled the aching mess onto the very "Chair of Phoenix," stretching to grab the article, crumbling it, and with a disgusted grunt, I deposited it into the trash can

Blades of Courage

Perched on the side of a dry mountain road

Emerges a luxuriant swatch of spring green grass

Amongst the dusty pebbles in the brazen,
scorching sun

No roots attached to search for the much needed,
life-giving moisture

Yet gently swaying joyously

It embraces the sweltering stagnant breeze

Courageously thriving life with no viable means

Of support yet humanity strives and searches

The world for the roots to ground the soul that

Aches for fulfillment

Searching for the life-sustaining moisture…

The destiny…

The reason…

For it all, without knowledge, like roots

Roots from which to cling to for support, for moisture, for life

Yet a smile emanates from within a well-groomed outer skin

But, on the inside, the struggle persists to sustain sanity without roots

And still, at this same moment

The vibrant appearance of the ambient grass

It emerges, without roots, to embrace the day

With wonder and excitement without fear of sustenance…it lives

Time passes and then another blade, tiny and sweet, gently swoons alongside its brethren

Indifferent to the struggle for survival

Both exhibiting the picture of health

From which they embrace the morning dew

When the Wash Basket Was Full

When the wash basket was full

Tiny pitter-patter of feet

Circled round my aching legs,

Dirty hands messed the walls,

Clattering pans smashed to the floor

When the wash basket was full

Sounds of unknown origin could be heard

Squeals of laughter muffled then whispers

As broken pieces lay scattered

Across the worn kitchen floor

Tiny Little Cracks

When the wash basket was full

Grumbling stomachs could be heard

Holes in pies surfaced unexpectantly

Buckwheat cracked cookies went missing

From grandma's chipped ceramic jar

When the wash basket was full

Peals of laughter filled the air

Freshly ripped Christmas paper

Lay shredded about

Smiles of gratitude came forth...

Salty tears fell...

When the wash basket was full

Silence was a precious peace

Never to be heard

Sleep fleeting and rare

Time was not present

Wishes for better yearned

When the wash basket was full

Dreams went unanswered

Days slipped by one by one

Until the day the wash basket stood empty